Somewhere Between Logic & Emotion

A book of poetry

By: Brandon Jackson

To My Lil' Sister, Crystal Jackson,
who has always been the day to my night.

I don't cry over spilled milk,
I smile over spilled wisdom,
That grows into oceans
Over time

Contents

Foreword

The Monomyth Model calls for the hero to venture forth in order to be molded into his or her potential for greatness.

In Brandon Jackson's journey, he personifies the call to adventure through harmonies that speak with empathy, with love, and with purpose. In *Somewhere Between Logic and Emotion*, he employs the written word to create a meaningful mix of metaphors to resonate with ideas that seem to come from an older spirit.

In this second venture, Jackson provides a supernatural word twist of melodious narrations that salve the spirit. I won't claim to know where the inspiration begins. I won't claim to be a part of that which inspires. I won't claim to do anything but encourage the person reviewing this foreword to spend time reading and reflecting through the pages and to claim for yourself that line that speaks to your need.

I won't claim to know how God is shaping this artist, but I will say that Jackson is well on his way through the transformation and on his way to atonement. His magic weapon, the pen, is simply unexplainable enjoyment.

Indeed. Throughout life people leave impressions. Brandon, I wish the Holy Spirit to continue moving about within your being and to keep providing the urge to write. Your words are heart on paper.

Peace and Blessings.

Yolonda (Yollie) Drawhorn
Writer. Teacher. Leader.
The Barack Obama Male Leadership Academy

Winter Poems

Loss. Loneliness. Realization.

Warnings

I'm usually the type that can always tell someone else
what's not good for them
But when it comes to me,
I'm not so intelligent

Last night, we did things
that our mothers would not be proud of but
I enjoyed the rebellion in our hands,
the virginity in your words and
the mischief that our limbs made
We shared weaknesses
That only pretend to be strong in the day
As my hormones prayed prayers
that you would answer them

You've got the kind of eyes,
people could get lost in
And the kind of lips that kiss poetry all over me
I loved the way your skin talked to me
And told me to cover it
with the graffiti in my fingerprints
Your mouth made promises
that sounded *alien* to me
Claiming that your intentions come in peace,
As the moon peeped like Tom and
Told us Tomorrow couldn't hear us,
Because reality doesn't hurt
when the stars are out
You've got the kind of face
That I've painted in my subconscious
Our moans were honest with each other and
Hopefully our bodies forgive us

for the marks we left on them
Because you've got the kind of hands
That draw passion in cursive
Last night, we tattooed each other
Like our tongues were needles
You've got the kind of arms
That could sweep the gravity from beneath me
The kind of scent,
that makes me drool for you
And the type of smile I could picture if I were blind
You've just got that something
That felt so good last night
To the point where I could be falling *hard* for you

But early this morning, your eyes are warning me
That they won't always look at me the same
Your touch is telling me
That there's nothing innocent about it
Your feet are warning me
That they've walked out on plenty of lives
So what makes me expect you wouldn't walk out on mine?
This morning, your mouth looks as if
it knows the perfect way to lie,
and your hands unraveled secrets
that they've ripped apart their share of hearts
So what makes me think you could protect mine?

This morning, it is your body language
That speaks out of selfishness and not selflessness
Then I notice,
You've got the kind of lips
that could blow people's worlds down
The kind of stare,
that could crush people's senses
So how many senseless things did you say last night
that haven't been said before?
How many ways did you feel me last night
that haven't been practiced before?
Maybe I'm just terrified

of what real love may feel like
But last night, you were a dream
And this morning, you are suddenly a warning sign
Convincing me to not hurt myself again

The sun makes you resemble
All of the mistakes I've made in the past
But last night, I knocked down walls for you
Just to prove that I could be brave enough to let you in
Now I'm second guessing the sound of your footsteps
But if I take the risk to enjoy you for the moment
Can you promise to continue what we felt last night?
Because early this morning
Your arms are warning me
That they won't be able
To. Hold. Me. Down.
Forever

Never Is A Very Long Time

The worst way to miss someone
Is knowing you could never hate them
Because hating them would be so much easier
than forgiving...
We screamed like
Echoes in grand canyons and
Hurt each other deep
Like black history
Still wanting forever
When forever said we couldn't handle it
I said I never wanted to see you again
But never is a very long time

The worst way to miss someone
Is not laying wide awake throughout the night,
It's actually falling asleep
Because sleeping brings the torture of good dreams
Chances to live things
That won't be there in the morning
I said never
But never is a very long time

The worst way to miss someone
Is placing that favorite picture in a frame
Having to swallow their name
Because you almost said it,
When you were in someone else's presence
Everyone wants a superhero
But we have to be okay with a little imperfection
Be careful in how we choose our companions and
Enjoy the time we had to sit at home with them
We pressure ourselves
To create a paradise that we don't even deserve yet
While we feel entitled to bliss,
We become confused within the arguments
Finding romance on TV screens

Angry that it won't translate to real life as easily

You said never,
But now never feels so much longer
Than the forever we said was worth fighting for
If everything was heaven,
I couldn't learn how to be strong when hell comes
Because it will come
To test the strength of a love you claim for someone

The worst way to miss someone
Is noticing how everyone after them
Can't seem to do the things you were used to
I've tried to teach people how to hug me a certain way
How to touch me, like a genius
How to support me, like a legend
How to have faith in me, like a miracle and
How to move me like the seasons move
Because if change is constant
Why can't love feel more like change?
We foolishly said never
And pride will make sure that we keep our word
Because the worst way to miss someone
Is thinking you can forget them
By what something sexual can promise you
Or how something creative can fulfill you
But denial will always leave you
Hungry

Everyone wants to be wanted
But who wants to be available
When it's time to be needed?
I so easily said never
But never is a very long time
Yet how could we even tell the difference
Because we were Never there
To lead love by example
And we were never there
To show Forever the great ways

people should love each other,
*(with **all** of our hearts,*
*And **less** of our minds)*
Because all Forever ever asked from us
Was just to give it
some
quality
time

Hoping Justice Will Call

I had hoped that
You were hiding in someone
who wanted to be the next President,
Making it evident that people with big hearts
Can run a country that can be so
heartless sometimes

I had hoped that
You were out ending disease and wars,
Protecting our children from
Zimmermans and drug lords
I had hoped that
You could one day polish America's reputation
Put love back in the water and
Iron out the wrinkles
In this crooked legal system

Dr. King said, "Let freedom ring"
So I waited in wee hours of the night
Beside my telephone,
Hoping that you, Justice, would call
Because I thought that in any relationship
Trust...was everything

See, I never asked you to save the world
Because a Savior and a Cross have already done that
But the least you could've done for me was *act*...
Like you cared
So instead of calling us back,
You just stared at mothers crying Armageddon tears
Never being truthful enough
to build confidence in our survival
Because you let so many freely,
Kill
A child

I was a child once,
Pledging allegiance to
One nation, under God, and indivisible
Do you even remember those promises of
with liberty and Justice...
For all?
I guess not
Because as I continue to sit by a *silent* phone
I remember again that liars
Never call

Commitment Is Dying

Ladies and Gentlemen,
We are in an age
Where kisses start in "I promise..."
But end in "I'm sorry..."
Marriage vows are turning into questions of
"How could you..."
And the answer we give is that
"Well, it's just a part of human nature..."
So while he's out sleeping with women familiar to her,
She'll call in a better man to construct kingdoms
And penetrate his freedom into her
Because how can you change a liar,
if lying is a culture?

Dearly beloved, we are gathered here today
To witness the infidelity
That we add to our grocery lists
And invite into our homes
Commitment is dying
And we are in a time
Where inhibitions freely fall
Around alcohol driven ankles
And fucking "accidentally"
Is a justifiable reason
For me to accept your apologies

From his breath,
she smelled another woman's soul
But she's already covered in another's fingerprints so,
it's all good
Because that's just the way it is
Commitment is dying
And a new world is approaching
Where the misogyny in today's music
Will become a young girl's proud mantra

Young boys will haunt her,
Saying, "I love you" just right
Because he'll follow in the footsteps of his father
When he walked out of his mother's life
This will be a world where
There will be no need for excuses
Just telling the truth of where we were last night
Deception will become an art form
And satisfaction will be defined by temporary bliss
Because for some reason, that temporary shit...
Feels so damn good

Maybe you think that my hands are too small
To handle the size of your insecurities
Or my imperfections must be too monstrous
For you to be fearless enough to stay
So when commitment completely dies,
I guess you won't have to hold back when
You get that urge to let me down
Cuz we're all grown
And grown people just have to learn to get over things, right?
I bet your eyes wouldn't be deep enough
To let me drown in them
Or better yet
I bet you couldn't teach me how to swim in them
Because nowadays disappointment
Is just supposed to happen, right?

At times, love will make you crawl back to Reality
Because reality is the only enemy that was always my friend
No matter how much I've been broken to the core,
I guess you couldn't help rebuild me
No matter how much I've been hurt to the bone,
I guess you couldn't help heal me
Commitment is dying
But it's so good that love is still surprising
Because one day, I want my pen to run its mouth about someone
I want my paper to spill secrets of how I feel about someone
I want the walls to hear me practice and prepare

For the very next time I'll speak to that someone
So could you make me call love mine again?
Could you be bold enough,
to have her reach cloud nine again?
Could you be brave enough to give him wings to fly again?
Because we've come entirely too far
Just to lose it
So whenever you say you're ready to love someone
Then I dare you, right now
To prove it

Woman of Steel

She wears concrete lipstick,
So his words won't penetrate when they kiss
Stone sits
in the corner
of her rib cage,
Persuading her heart to give up its position…
There is iron in her touch,
And metal in her eyes
Her hands are made of **BRICKS**
Building barricades strong enough
So another man
can never
kick it down again
She dreams in solid **ICE**
Because it's cold going to sleep alone at night
But she cements those memories as the morning
Tries to melt her insecurities away…
Her mouth is made of wood now
Where her bark is worse than her bite
Abandoning the smile she once had…
Her skin is like glass
Where you can see old fingerprints
Left by failed relationships
But her anger
allows them
to be transparent
She is now… a **WOMAN OF STEEL**
Not the superhero,
Just a body full of attitude that can bruise your confidence,
As her words hit like rocks
She'd rather…
Walk on hot coal…
Than walk into possibilities with you
But she used to be
As soft as a child's cheek
There used to be

Diamonds in her teeth when she'd laugh and
Her love,
Oh, her love was pure Gold
As her skin dripped sweet copper over her lover's tongue
Her body was bronze and
Her style made silver jealous,
Because she never tainted, was never rusted
Until she trusted in someone
She cried mercury tears that poisoned her pillow cases
Her self esteem folded into paper,
After pain stretched into skyscrapers
No statue of liberty, she's a statue of regret
So now
she hates
all men
Promising herself to never be sown into cotton
Made to dress them
No one can hold her
Cuz she's way too hard
No one can feel her
Cuz she's way too distant
And no one can talk to her
Unless walls could talk back
But maybe if she built something with another,
She'd be able to tear her own walls down,
And have a patience that no one else likes to try
I hope she'll be prepared one day,
When her mind changes and
When the heart relapses into someone else's lap
Who will show her that *protecting* yourself,
doesn't mean closing yourself
And that *loving* yourself,
Means allowing others who want to love you, love you
She refuses to be broken
But we all have our pieces missing
And no matter how strong her steel is now
Real love
Can crack
Anything

I Fall In Love With Broken People

I used to never believe in parallel universes
But I often wonder
Where else could we have misplaced
the common sense that Heaven gave?
Take me for example
I fall in love with broken people
Who leave their tears behind like bread crumbs,
just trying to find a way back home...
The kind who are content with sailing on sinking ships
And who find happiness in bad habits...
People who promise that they'll never hurt me,
Like the world hurt them...
They lied

I fall in love with homeless individuals
Who find welcome mats in my kindness,
Who become false disciples to my needs,
Who speak in flexible fairy tales
That stretch far beyond the truth
The kind who are sensual with their eye stares and
Deadly by the touch of a hand
People who seem to understand me
As if they were God's co-creator
Yet I'm always there
To hold their heads just above water
Even though I've never learned
how to swim...

I fall in love with dreamless sleepers
Preying off my loneliness
As I slave to set their nightmares free
See, my love has superhero qualities
It'll save you from burning buildings and
Rescue you from regret
It'll multitask with healing your wounds
And do favors without you having to ask

It will give everything
Without requiring anything,
in return...

I fall in love with hurt people who hurt people
Those who carry bags of excuses to why
They decorate Rock Bottom
To be as comfortable as possible
Yet I become more than willing,
To lay my head there too

I grow attached to people with cracks in their security
Shared bedsides and dreams with
Angelic/demons,
Sweet/bitterness,
Trustworthy/liars,
Wonderful/pain,
Healing/diseases,
Strong/weaknesses
And some intelligent/stupidity
Damn, what a dangerous sanctuary,
Our friend Ignorance can be
Because I had to learn that
Giving YOU selfless love
Does not mean
Loving myself LESS
Yet every day I accommodate love
To those who should've learned about it growing up
I am the crutch for those who feel like
Life is just too heavy to walk through
So I sacrifice my balance
In order to travel beneath them
So they know what standing tall feels like

I fall in love with broken people
With no time for soul searching
Praying to be reconnected with purpose
But never wanting their priorities fixed
For some reason,

Hurt people love to love hurt people
So while some may not believe in a parallel universe
I often picture another world
Where we must be walking proud and confident
Around a knowledge that is heaven sent
Because we don't walk like that here
This would be a world where
We are scarred by several, but never broken by anyone
Flawed by nature, but knowing that we are perfectly created by Grace
This would be a world where
We all would know the difference
Between the love, we carry
And the love, we waste

Spring Poems

Sunshine. Love. Infatuation.

Scared

True love, you don't walk into it
You stumble
But I'm scared of falling
Not sure whether to call you clueless or insane
Because how could anyone have found a safe place
In loving a disaster like me...

You lend me refuge in your smile,
which is the best piece of architecture I know,
I evacuate to your arms
When the storms get too hard to handle
Because your soul is different
A love so sufficient
That with you, I couldn't be a child anymore

I couldn't use insecurities as crutches
I'd have to grasp responsibility
With you, I couldn't sit and write no amateur poetry
I'd have to get as deep as you and
Stand as strong as your backbone
I'd feel like I'd want to take care of someone
Who needs no taking care of
Teach someone who knows everything already
Love someone who loves enough for the universe
So what use could I ever be to you?

The childish parts of me,
Would have to drop dead
In order to love something so drop dead gorgeous
I'd have to fit into maximum proportions to impress you
Dig deep into emotions
So I could be bold enough to protect you
I couldn't just caress you
By the hand, no
Because it takes an intangible touch to massage you just right

You inspire transformation
Communication so sweet that
There were pieces left in our teeth
And flossed out in our kisses
But I've never shared lips like this
Never had out of body experiences like this
Your heart is on the table
But what would I do with a love like this?

It's scary
To have to tell the demons in my bed
That they have to find somewhere else to sleep
Or evict the skeletons from my closet
To make room for your shoes next to mine
I'd have to get myself together
In order to love you better
But the fear in me sees 1st Corinthians
As just an opinion...
Because the fact is, putting away childish things
Brings too much space for reality

If fear were not here, I wouldn't love you to death
I'd love you to life
If fear were not here
I wouldn't steal the value
from how rewarding it feels to *earn* someone priceless
If fear were not here,
I'd be the floor to welcome your knees
As you prayed for the strength of us combined
If fear were not here,
I'd blow away your tears like dandelion petals
If fear were not here,
I'd be enslaved to love you
Because I should be the image of how much you deserve it

But I'm scared of you
Not because I think you would leave me
But because I know you would change me
And I'm scared

Of genuinely liking the person
That I could become

Our Daughters' Hands

If I ever have a daughter
I'd teach her hands how to be stronger than others
No, they wouldn't be big, rough, or ugly
They'd be firm enough to balance things
That the world expected to be too heavy for her
Her hands
Would have enough muscle in them
To hold the weight of this human heart

As a curious little girl,
Her finger might touch the top of a hot stove,
Which would be the first time she'd learn
How life can burn you unexpectedly...
But I wouldn't fuss
I'd just place her hand under some cold running water
Where she would then understand how it feels to heal

As a teenager
I'd teach her how to grip reality
Never allowing her to live in the fantasy of
Palm readings or crossed fingers for luck
Because that shit just doesn't work
When it comes to the real hurt
Of loving a man for what he could be
Rather than realizing the man that he is
My daughter's hands would know what to hold onto
And when to let go of what she sometimes will fear losing

As an adult
She'd know how to wave goodbye to painful relationships,
Welcome happiness with open arms
She'd caress her pillows at night with a smile of patience
Waiting on the right hand of a man
Or woman to embrace hers
She'll produce art with her hands, just like her father
She'd be an author of existence

Reaching for galaxies that she'd inherit after me

I'd teach her hands how to take control of her future
Never allowing someone to drive it for her
Because she'd be the captain of the wheel and
God would be her direction
She'd be able to recognize history in her skin
DNA that came from the hands of great ancestors
So her hands could open doors and turn pages
To explore the consciousness of reaching others,
Feeling her way across life lessons and
Expanding her prints across the continents

My daughter's hands would drop sexist expectations and
Throw away racist standards
She'd possess countless gifts to give to the empty handed
Never taking what she'll never need
It would be a blessing to shake her hand
Because a woman's ability to hold, to have and to love
Is constantly battered and beaten
Scarred and bruised
Scorned and broken
Tainted and used
But my daughter's hands would emulate the hands of a king
Because she would've mastered being a queen very early
And although her hands would get dirty
She'd know how to wash them in prayer
Catch her tears
And watch them dry as a part of experience
Because in this world, she'd have to be smarter
Have to be tougher, have to be stronger
In order to be happy longer
So until she's born, until it's that time
I make the promise today
That my daughter will learn that kind of strength
That only God
Can design

It Would've Been Nice To Like You

It would've been nice to like you...
For life to be elementary again,
For smiling to be as natural as breathing,
Where numbers grow tired of being countless
in the moments I'd think of you...
I'd count the hairs on your head,
if you gave me the time to,
Reinvent the alphabet
So every word and sound would bow down to the way
we'd speak them...
I'd be speechless, if you wanted to fill in the blanks
Make arts and crafts in our privacy
Easily turn four walls into lessons of geography
Because we could travel the world in our home
Discover new lands on our skin
It would've been nice to love you
For love to be simple again,
For my touch to color within the lines of you
As our tongues drew in cursive,
Make love geometrically until we were shapeless,
Speak fluently in that language called Passion
It would've been nice to fight for the cause together
Be adults but still grow up together
Be childish so we could laugh together
Be lovers, so we could conquer all together
Yeah, it would've been nice
But realistically,
You like to live in crossword puzzles and
Give signals that point over the edge of mountains
You speak to me in less than paragraphs
And sometimes less than sentences
I guess consistency is only for the scientists to figure out
Since obviously commitment is a sort of calculus and
Affection, a kind of algebra
Promises are not your word problems
You shouldn't make them, if you can't solve them

Because now it would only take surgery
To learn what's inside of you
I'd have to conquer equations
To find out if we are equal or not
Read novels to see if we're still on the same page
Show you how to tie your shoes
So you'll stop tripping over your words
See I'm not with that puppet shit
If you find it amusing in stringing me along
I'm not with that unintelligent shit
Willing to dumb myself down for you
I shouldn't have to research your reasons
For not stating your intentions
IN
PLAIN
ENGLISH
Or write a thesis about how much God intended love to work
Because it shouldn't have to be explained
Just lived
Love is simple
But it's not for the simple minded
Yes, it would've been nice to try this again
But I just don't have time
To teach...
Children

Writer's Block (A Happy Poem)

I have writer's block
Because I may be in love
You make me speechless
With a laziness in my fingers
Because instead of picking up pens
I'm too busy running them
through your hair…
You give me ideas too big to fit on paper and
A spoken word too difficult to understand
So my performance is through my heartbeat
rather than through my hands
I savor the rhythm you give me through my laughter
Because you make me smile in a way that Michael Angelo couldn't paint and
Make me feel a feeling that Shakespeare couldn't stage

I think I have writer's block
Because now disappointment is afraid of me,
when it used to be my greatest inspiration
Lately, I haven't cried enough
To build words from the water wasted from late nights
Because now I spend late nights
Watching you, watch me
And it's something beautiful about the way you see me
Now I'm greedy
Never full from your kisses
As they refresh me like lemonade
Placed over scars that were opened when
I'd write about things like heartache
But when the wounds heal,
Poetry can take a break
No need to be written or spoken when it's in motion
As we make music in the morning and
Create weather in the evening time
We have thunderstorm passion
As summer time happens right in between the sheets

I've whispered in your ear
In ways that made my microphone jealous
And my notebook pages cry out for my tear stains
Because now all I draw in them are smiley faces
With my signature next to yours
I've told you secrets without the metaphors
And knew there was a talent in your lips
When you expressed how those secrets made you love me more

I must have writer's block
Because I can't write sad poems
I can't find the chips
You knocked off my shoulders and
You cater to the emotions
That were once like leeches on my sleeves
You climbed over walls
I never intended on destroying
Having no choice but to enjoy the luxury of resting in someone's eyes
again
Because my dreams let me know how genuine your arms are
It feels good to be brave with you and
It feels good to crave you and
It feels good to witness promises that don't break
But actually fulfill themselves
Because you're preparing me to write something
I haven't written in a long time
Poetry inspired from happiness

I thought it was writer's block
But I realized God didn't take His gift from me
He just gives it to me everyday
In another form

Metaphors

(To those who made promises and left them at my doorstep)

You said that I was your adventure
And you wanted to take time in traveling me...
So I stood wide open,
The moment you said that the ground we'd walk on
would be made of the same air we'd breathe....
Because you said you'd have me
floating

You compared me to things that made me feel like
I was literature incarnate,
Told better than any story book pages,
As we had the passion of teenagers
Believing we had it all under control.
So into your soul, I just felt like
Pain was yesterday and
Forever could start tomorrow
As I'd find forgiveness in your metaphors
Because you were a religion
And I followed you
faithfully

You were influential like young memories
That made me fearless of getting older
Symbolically refreshing,
Every time you'd claim that I was the one you were meant for
I fell in love with your metaphors
Cuz it was something gravitational about the way you'd say
Baby, let's move these mountains together
Or how you said I was made of steel
But you were confident that your love could crack me

You told me
to not fight your floods
Because they were meant to wash me,

since I was used to wrestling oceans
You said that if I just flowed with you,
I could be your Atlantic
Yes, your lips were specific
Never giving a stutter or a speechless moment
You said that I was the celebrity
who made your dreams famous
As I told you, you were a savior to my vision
And a soldier for my feelings
Remembering how you promised to protect my heart
That was so used to loving contradictions...

I've never fallen in love with a Poet
But I've loved people whose promises sounded like Poetry
Sometimes metaphors are all you have to hang on to
Especially, when that someone disappears
And all you hear are the beautiful things they told you,
in order to keep your ignorance warm...
You used to make us sound beautiful
But actually being beautiful became hard for us to do

I think the only downside to *being* a Poet
Is that I love words too much
I've dealt with the creative ways they paint pictures
from lips I would've died for
Promising me the world
When you can't afford the soil to grow us in
And there's nothing metaphorical
About the nights that were heavy without you
There's nothing symbolic
About the distance you showed me
Once you weren't into me like you used to be

I put my heart on the line
For your analogies and figurative languages
As you put your heart and soul into your words
And never into your actions
But see I didn't need all of your decorative sentences
All you had to do was tell me...
That you've found inspiration in someone else
Because the moment I promised time,
That I'd never waste it again...
That's when your words sounded the most convincing

I think my addiction is
I fall in love with the potential that I saw from the beginning
During those days of metaphorically speaking
But next time, I don't want to be impressed
With what someone thinks is the best thing to say
Because sometimes it's not about the things you'd put into Poetry
It's about you being straight-forward with me
And in doing that
We could've loved each other,

Literally

Love Me Like...

How do you love a complex person, simply?
How do you love a complex person, simply?
This is how

Love me like young memories at old ages
Like children turning storybook pages
Love me like teenagers love control
Like a heart to soul music
Give me just a remnant of your thinking
To occupy a space that is reserved to think about me
Love me like minutes and hours, todays and tomorrows
Give me yesterday wishes to relive it
Love me like time loves eternal
Like heat loves to be cooled down or
Cold loves to be warmed up
Love me like the sun holds up blue canvases
For our faces to be painted in
Love me like an artist and his inspiration
A poet and her creativity
Like a butterfly's symmetry
Like streams search for that ocean to merge with
Love me in rainbow colors
Love me in infinite numbers
Like rocket science and simple math
Love me like lungs love breathing
Or hearts love beating
Love me for the message within me
For you were created to listen to it
Love me like Obama loves hope
Like the same loves change
Like ears long for certain words
And like tears have pathways for cleansing hurt
Love me like a little sister to her big brother
Like a father to his only daughter
Love me like a summer breeze against skin
Like you'll never love again

Love me like a religion
Like Psalms and Proverbs
Love me in spiritual and scientific terms
Love me like a Savannah thirst drinking water
Like the galaxy harbors the stars of our birthdays
Rebirth my day just by being near me
Loving me like my dreams can hear me
Share me with preschool faith and adult ambition
Mention me to your goals
And see if I can be a part of them
Love me like fingerprints against glass
Like questions loved to be asked
Be my answer to this mystery of companionship
Love me like our grandparents' relationship
Love me like words written in permanent ink
Never removing the
Permanently marked impression you've made on me
Love me like sweaty, passionate, thunderstorm love
Like arms holding a newborn love
Love me like ice cold lemonade
Made to refresh my energy that's willing to move just for you
Love me like a child's band aid
Where hearing your name is enough medicine for me
Love me for what love isn't
Instead of figuring out what love is
Love me like first kiss love
Like God so loved the world love
I want you to love me like souls love eternity
So I ask again
How do you love a complex person, simply?
How do you love me, simply...?

This is how

Summer Poems

Heat. Truth. Imperfections.

Their Secret

I can't believe that my grandmother
Still has that twinkle in her eye
When she looks at him
Or how my grandfather could still conquer wars with his smile
When he touches her….
This is the aftermath of love,
the actual continuance of forever,
When the storms of 50 plus years have subsided and
The world…
Really doesn't matter to them anymore
As they've spawned generations to continue their legacy

I've never lived the meaning to,
till death do us part,
For better or for worse,
Through sickness and in health
Never truly knew what God meant when He said,
Love is patient,
Love is kind
Until I took the time to witness, this ageless connection
I wish *we* could be more like them…
But the era of love has changed
I wonder what's their secret…

Take us for example,
IT'S JUST WAAAAAY TOO DIFFICULT TO HAVE
THAT KIND OF SUCCESS
WITH ANOTHER PERSON!
I could NEVER see me loving you SO unconditionally that…
It was almost the way God feels about you…or
Accept you BEYOND your imperfections,
Listen to your days of insecurities,
Learning from the pain you endured before me,
So we can spend nights healing the wounds together

I should be able to place you as my reflection,

See every part of me that you understand,
Because I'd remember our relationship
From past lifetimes
That you could find genetically coded in our fingerprints
Your presence should resuscitate me *every* morning…
I should fall in love with the movement of your sound waves,
the ones that musically perform my name,
Which I'd thank my mother for giving me everyday
Because you say it perfectly

We should never get tired of each other
We should grow OLD and feel AGELESS
Kept young by complimenting our spirits and
Beautifully patterned to create symmetry SO ancient…
They'd try to place it in history
But realistically…

We rather create **HURRICANES** and
Just ride the waves until they drift us apart
We taint our happily ever after with our selfishness
And stain our motivations to intentionally hurt each other,
Because someone got hurt first
I don't think I could really be there when you need me
I go mute when you cry to me
You go deaf when I call to you
We blame each other for our faults
Taught ourselves how to shut out new possibilities and
Replace the lonely
With something to temporarily make us feel complete
I don't think…we could ever learn their secret
How to put patience in our practice
Plant seeds of promises that won't grow and then die
just because it's winter,
But plant a love that knows how to last all year round
Our vows should sound like
I, WANT TO OUTLAST STORMS LIKE MY ELDERS
I, WANT TO KEEP THAT SMILE
THAT DOESN'T CRACK FOR DECADES TO COME
I, WANT TO MELT IN THAT TOUCH THAT NEVER GROWS OLD

I, WANT THAT MYTH, THAT LEGEND
OF AN EMOTION THEY SAY CONQUERS ALL
I, SHOULD BE SUBJECT TO LOVE EVERY DETAIL OF YOU
I, WILL LOVE YOU DESPITE OF...
I, WILL LOVE YOU REGUARDLESS...
I, WILL LOVE YOU ANYWAY...
AND I WILL LOVE YOU NONNTHELESS...

But who am I kidding...
We could never,
Love each other,
Like that

Could we

"Great Men"

(For the corrupt politicians, policemen, preachers, and so on)

These kinds of "great men"
Hate men
Who aren't like them
Instead of save men,
These pretend to be saints men
Rather cage men and
Enslave men
Engrave names of men who look like me
To tombstones
Since the poor
Don't praise these men

These great men sleep in
Comfortable linens
These fake men,
Move like snake men
These eating steak men,
Make men and then break men
While pretending to be brave men

These highly paid men, fade men
Who are not wealthy like them
These aged men,
Do not aid men
They just play men,
Of high intelligence
Great men, pay men,
Send in replaced men
To do their dirty work
They frame men, and then blame men
But state men are all equal
Secretly,
They bait men, erase men
These want you to fail men,
Place men in prison

Rather than educate men

These great men, face sin
Believing there's none within them
These great men, don't pray for men
They hate gay men
Because they say straight men
Are the only great men
These heartless clay men,
Molded in images to sway men
Beat men and kill men
Send in police henchmen
To intimidate men

These great
Politician Men
Claim to be great
Christian Men
But still hate men,
Who aren't like them

God, I wish we could mutate men,
From these so called great men
I wish we could trade small thinking men,
For some big loving men
These all about the gain men,
For some praying men
Then maybe we could train men,
To not be ashamed in
Standing up for what's Right
For the life of every Hu-man
I want to see real great men
Draped in
Nothing but Wisdom

Man, what a great world that would be
Without these "Great men"
These take and take and take men,
These United States Men...

A Bittersweet Confession

In this type of circumstance,
I wish roses were red
And violets were blue
But in this lifetime,
The roses have been bleeding
While the violets cry
Because this isn't that type of happy poem
More like...bittersweet
See, love shouldn't only have to live in dreams
Because it should never be forbidden
I've already given my heart to someone
Who has recently forgotten how to treat it
And that's when you came along,
Who realized what I needed
We say we'll see each other next lifetime
But the anticipation makes every day another lifetime
Somehow, you redefine a passion that I've lost
And your touch keeps the definition replaying
We pretend like, we have no one else to go home to
Held hands like, wedding rings were not visible
Even exchanged the taste of each other's lips,
As if they weren't already spoken for
And it's always bittersweet, when we meet again
As much as I love seeing you,
I always hate it at the same time
Because in my dreams, we are together
But in reality, we could never be
So today, all we can do is play house
But tonight, we'll go back to the ones we've made promises to
The one I call soul mate
Yet my soul is complete, with you...
I don't think I can be brave anymore
Because the hand that gets to occupy yours
Is starting to scare me
It's getting harder to be stronger anymore

Because I'm not the one to break up families
So I'll have to let you go
But I promise to whisper about you, in my prayers
Hoping the one I sleep next to, doesn't hear
Then I'll close my eyes and imagine,
And maybe even shed a tear
Because as easy as letting you go seems
Love shouldn't only have to live in dreams...

Closure

I come back to you,
Like an unfinished poem
Despite knowing that I did the best I could
I run back to you,
Like an unfinished poem
Because I just can't write an ending to you
That I can truly feel comfortable with

A Beautiful That's Not Mainstream

You took the time to get to know me
In chronological order
Now...that's beautiful
And not the kind that you see on television screens,
You are single father raising his children beautiful
Young inner city kids graduating school beautiful
I've witnessed similar pain in you
Defeated death in your embrace
While you act as if, caring for me
Is a career for you
Now...that's beautiful
And not the kind they depict in music
You are young girl waiting for the right one,
at the right time beautiful
Dark skinned women proud of their melanin beautiful
See, this life sometimes gives you a universe to travel alone in
But I've grown in your wounds
As you've uplifted my spirits
Announced forgiveness like God's tongue and
Taught me that hurt will introduce you to completion, eventually
Now...that's beautiful
And not the kind you've seen in magazines
You are equal rights beautiful
HIV cure beautiful
I have given up on trying to tame wild rivers
Instead, I let the fearlessness in your arms be my still waters
Because you hold me with such assurance,
whenever I start to doubt
So now let me tell you why you're beautiful
There was nothing ever condescending in your words
Never any stigma in your eyes
You never had any expectations
To what love is supposed to look like
There was never any exploitation in your intentions
Never any greed in your fingers
Or high pedestals in your attitude

You didn't have to sign a contact
In order to love me back
Now that's beautiful
Defined not by what is visible to the eye
But by what's created through honesty
History lessons of unconditional love
In order to make love unconditional again
Within the lines of poetry, readers will find us,
if they look hard enough
I was born into this world, crying
Knowing there would be times
Where the only choice is to be brave
And I have to say
That the journey to you was worthwhile
I know this
Because from the beginning
When I told you I was imperfect
You decided to love me regardless
Now this is beautiful
And not the kind you'll see posted
on billboards

Pray For Our Children

Absent fathers,
You are making them
Make-believe in you
Angry mothers,
You are not protecting them from nightmares
When you are too busy dwelling in your own
See, the monsters are no longer under the bed
They are roaring from the radio stations,
Placing deception in storybook beats.
There are assassins in our school districts
And evil trolls in our Congress
Destroying bridges and the villages it takes
To raise those who have the potential to accomplish
Anything

Please pray for our children
Because there are fairytales on television screens
Dictating their definitions of beautiful
There are pretty colors in the drugs and
Candy coated street corners
That our young boys are drooling for
There are lies in our justice system and
Violence in our homes
There is contradiction in our churches and
Stones that are breaking their spirits
There is prejudice in our statistics and
Skeletons in our closets
That we give away as hand me downs
There are predators as our neighbors
And henchmen in our movie theaters
Our youth are taking instructions from
Rappers with sesame street names,
Pawns and victims of their own generational curses,
To influence the death of change
I wish someone would've prayed harder for them
Because we are still living slave pain

That is so boldly present

Remember that our children are like sponges
Young girls absorb the water cried out by their mothers
Only to be recreated when young men
Want to squeeze the living tears out of her
How I long for grandmothers' singing
To be their lullabies at night
How I yearn for grandfathers' stories
To be their direction in life
We are here to provide broad shoulders to carry them on
And a strong back to take the lashes
So our descendants will not be beaten, swallowed,
and regurgitated
By a world that has Mother Nature
But has never owned a mother's nature

We are here to put down the toys and instill the truth
Like gifts under trees during every season
Teaching our children to not only dream during bedtime
But to dream all day long
Be the example for our sons to stop building playgrounds and
Invest in kingdoms
Teach our teenagers that it's okay to make mistakes
But to learn from the hangovers
Even if you have to choke on memories that sometimes linger
Like second hand smoke
Confide in them to be able to find their own way home
When we leave this Earth and are called home ourselves
Now how beautiful does that sound
And how beautiful would that look
If we held onto our children a little tighter, everyday
I'm thankful for my mother who still prays for me
Who taught me since I was a little boy
That God has never been and will never be
an imaginary
friend

Fall Poems

Change. Movement. Healing.

Balance Haiku

Today was windy
No matter how hard it blew
I didn't fall once

My "Where Have You Been All My Life"

After the
cold sheets and sleepless nights,
Where the stars laughed at my loneliness
Because they had company, while I had none
After the
Never calling me back,
When someone said they would and
After the never meeting me halfway,
When someone said they could
After wondering whose scent
was frequently brought home to me...
My only question now is,
Where have *you* been all this time?

After every lie, I was looked right in the eye with,
After every face that grew more unfamiliar as time spent,
After good intentions were enlisted as promises,
After their sentences looked sexy in uniform,
After being convinced that someone's words
could overshadow contradictions,
After I believed them and
After I grieved when
Listening was never popular to them,
After all the selfishness that never sees
Two people in relationships,
After the ignorance that longs for love
But never understands how to keep it...
I just want to know
Where have *you* been, during all of this?

When bullshit was plentiful,
After the remarkable timing
When the very moment I was almost over someone,
Became the same moment I'd fall back in love with them
After all of the acting
Was done to perfection

And after the tears they poured
Came out so convincing,
After their stares were so photogenic
With a thousand reasons
To why loving them was worth repeating,
All I want to know is...
Where have *you* been hiding?

During the times that love made me feel like nothing and
The times I cried out everything,
When rock bottom was comfortable
And when I was only inspired to write
Angry, sad, heartbreaking poems,
almost forgetting how writing used to be an enjoyable thing,
After all of the people who left me loveless,
At what distance did you see me
Deciding to show up
And whisper in my ear, that I am good enough?

Because since you've come along,
The sheets are never cold
Just heavy and warm with the scent of how passion
Is supposed to work
No cloud nine here,
You brought reality with you
I've found someone who appreciates my company enough
To never have the stars laugh at me again
But make them jealous
Of how someone shines brighter with me
I noticed, that you would've never fit into my design perfectly
Until after it was broken
Caressing the cracks in me, until they completely closed
I never imagined asking someone,
"Where have you been all my life?"
Until I realized that walking in wrong direction,
can sometimes lead you to where you're supposed to be

I want to thank the ones
Who broke me down

So someone could build me up
Because now there's a trust that's just natural enough
For this person who returns my phone calls
Just to share how their day went,
For this person who was sent
To make peace of the war written on my face and
Convince my heart that it's okay to beat hard
Because it's no longer scared to break
Someone who is the first thought of each day
And the destination of my nighttime
Someone who took all the regret away and
Gave me honesty, spoken honestly
Showed me a destiny, destined early
The definition of Patiently
Is what I almost missed
And now I can thank all of my heartbreakers
For leading me to this
And I have to say it's...
Been such a mean world
Without you

More N Words

Nnnnnnever
Nnnnnnnnnnothing
Nnnnnnnowhere
Nnnnnnnigga!

Nnnnnno One
Nnnnnnnot
Nnnnnnnnnnever
Nnnnnnnnnigga!

Nnnnnnnno
Nnnnnnnnneither
Nnnnnnor
Nnnnnnnnnnnnnigga!

See these are more N words that hurt
More N words that they define us with,
Deprive us with,
Hypnotized us with
So we accept Nigga as our term of endearment
But if that is so, then where do we place the other N words
That they see as synonyms
When they think or say,
You'll Never be
Nothing
Nigga...

Little black boy
Young black man
Throw your strong hands in the air
So God can raise you up
Throw them high
Before they lose their freedom in handcuffs,
or become replaced by angel wings
when you are chased by neighborhood watchmen

There's a whole kingdom
That they've tried to scratch your name from, but
Never compromise the crown you are bound to
Now I know drowning in negativity
Can make it feel clinically impossible to think positive
And how could anyone ever expect you to bleed out
all of the slave pain that our veins
still carry?

You may have your own opinions
About N words and their definitions
But I learned a long time ago in English class
That you shouldn't use double negatives
in your sentences
So little black boy
Put down that Nothing
and pick up Anything
Put down that Never
and pick up Right Now
Put down that Nowhere
and pick up Everywhere
Put down that No
And pick up Yes, Yes, Yes
Put down that Neither
And pick up All
Put down that Not
And pick up Can
Put down that word Nigga
and pick up Man
Because you are everything more
And nothing less
Than a child of God
And a reflection
Of His best

In The Blink... Of An Eye

In the blink of an eye,
I've seen people hitchhiking in night skies,
Trying to find their way back to daydreams
Because somewhere along the way,
We have forgotten that we are stars
I've seen us lose todays and
Waste tomorrows
Carrying carelessness on our shoulders
Because our shine was stolen
In the blink of an eye,
I saw what we could've been and could've had
But settled for scarred fairytales
With the stench of cliché smells
Time is compelled to shrink, not by the minute
But in the blink of an eye,
So I played staring games with reality
Thinking I could win some mercy
Yet still made decisions without foundation
In the blink of an eye,
I reevaluated life when death showed me it was real
We sacrifice eternal for temporary things
Deemed rulers over lustful things
As man sells his lies to women's thighs and
Her heart sells her trust to his hands
Damn, HIV spreads like forest fires
Death salts ocean wounds in our communities
In the blink of an eye,
I sat and watched brain waves die
As they try to advertise No Hope
Some Christians coast along in the motion of Sunday sermons
But Monday through Saturday, they judge me
Putting their so called righteousness on hold
No patience to think, we just act
And now it's time for judgment
But where did all the mornings go
When sunrise used to come with those second chances?

I could've been doing something bigger
Something good, something better
But in the blink of an eye,
Rock bottom pulls angels from the sky
Who sold their wings for some sex, some drugs,
Or some popularity
Disease makes us think that God is suddenly out of business
So we took our faith to the hospitals
To be reworked, hoping they take our prayers as insurance
Sometimes it happens that quick,
Love is disrespected
As we take smiles for granted
In a drop of a dime
I was penniless and
Rainy days came more often
It happens that quick
Bullets killing generations in front of me
Prisons confining men who look like me and
Politicians destroying what love and choice believe in
It happens that quick
Tears stitched to memories
Where hearts were broken faster than
Our young daughters having daughters and
Immature boys becoming fathers
Our legacy could die in the blink of an eye
If we let it,
So we should keep choosing life
Instead of choosing to regret it
Because if we're not willing to save it
It'll continue to happen that quick...
Murder, Infidelity, War, Poverty
Disease, Deception, Loss, Aggression
A continuum of wrong direction
See life happens as quickly as we blink our eyes
And it hurts sometimes, but we have to hold on to it
No matter how much it shakes us
As pain happens fast,
The sweetest Changes can take us years
And if we keep sleeping...

We might miss that day
When Change is here

As God Is My Witness

As God is my witness
I'll never settle for a love that is impatient
Or a love that is unkind
I'll stop trying to find heaven in someone's eyes
Or compare their touch to an angel's voice
Because that's how I always fall for imitations
Their embrace will never be my religion
I'll do my best to stop finding refuge in their kisses
Or believe their words to be prophetic images
Because they have no weight to them
Instead, they just rain down like fallen angels
And I end up blessed with problems that I never prayed for
As God is my witness
There will be no more Sabbath in their bedroom
I won't fast and pray from missing them
While hoping that starving myself from something better
Will somehow make this work...
I promise to not seek salvation in their promises
Or expect miracles from their hands
Because those are the same hands that keep me waiting...
But as God is my witness, I'm only human
And their smile is as tempting as the tree of good and evil
They bare me fruits of hope,
while they promise to never crucify me
I must admit, their whispers on my neck felt holy
And their arms opened up like pearly gates
That led me down golden streets when I was lonely
See, they gave me permission...
To think that I could walk on water with them
I created worlds in a week with them
Rode in chariots and parted skies
I crossed deserts and conquered countries with them
I found Jordan in their tears
And Jerusalem in their skin
Because something about them was just
Testimonial and

Hell didn't scare me when it was tricked into looking beautiful
So convinced that a God-like love
Could come just as easily from a human
But as God is my witness
I'll never again think that forever can be built from lips
Or believe that a savior can be born from a bad relationship
From now on, I'll accept real rainbows
Promising to never drown my world again
And as God is my witness
I'll witness real love and
Forgive them for hurting me, as I thank them for teaching me
To never put my faith
In someone who says they can take the loneliness away
But give it to who can instill the knowledge
That love never leaves you alone in the first place

I Fasted You Today

I didn't dial your number
That has always been easy to remember,
I turned every picture of you backwards,
Ignored your sweet text messages and
Your nonchalant voicemails
I didn't dream of you when I took a nap,
Drove everywhere but to your place,
Watched television,
Never seeing your face
I weaned myself from your familiar pacifying voice,
Broke through my annoying shell of tolerance,
See, I didn't hurt in silence today
I was loud in laughter
Washed my clothes freely in experience
That was dirty with broken heart residue on the sleeves
And tears that no longer believed in your shoulders
I received change today,
Saw sunshine through the rain today,
I stopped loving you, stopped living you
And I stopped hurting over you today
I prayed about everything
That didn't involve relationships
Took trips to good food, good friends and good music
I listened to songs
that didn't remind me of we or us
Put my trust in Him who has never hurt my feelings
I meditated on loving myself today,
Cleaned my desires for pain today,
Cleared my direction to happiness today,
I dressed to impress me today,
My heart beat for me today,
My mind thought for me today
And life had all of my attention
I never even mentioned you today
And tonight, when I laid down without you
I didn't cry for you, or because of you

It was one of the best feelings I've had in a while
Almost forgot how it felt
I figured out how to care for myself today
And you know what?
I think I'll do the same thing
Tomorrow

Love Advocate

Someone once told me
"Brandon, you love like you come from a loveless household."
And then I asked, how so?

That's when they told me,
"You love like last chance love,
A begging kind like children pleading with fathers
to stay for a while
You give a tolerating kind of love,
Like battered women's faces okay with purple-black roses
That grow best underneath the eye
Because of the tears that water them there.
You love with an ignorant type of optimism,
and a preschool type of ambition
That makes you trust when it's not earned.
You love like, you've learned how to accept Liars growing up
You love weak like young girls
Whose validation never came easy
Now trying to find replacement daddies in boyfriends
You love strong like young men
Raised in the quality time of unlit streets,
searching for a mother's love to soften the concrete.
You give addiction love,
As if needles, pipes, and spoons were afternoon hobbies
that you witnessed your family take part in
You give emotional love,
Like you had a father
Who must've stomped or beat the MAN out of you
You give such sacrificial love,
Like you had a mother chastise the Jesus out of you
You love like she never told you
Or like your father never showed you
You love like you come from a loveless household
Because those who were broken
Tend to love like you do...
And you give it blindly sometimes,

Even desperately sometimes..."

So then I told Mr. and Mrs. Someone,

"My mother has always been the Goddess kind,
Who laid foundations of what Love is and isn't,
Who God assured me
That by touching the hem of her garment,
There would never be that broken kind
And despite my father's mistakes
I've learned about that forgiving kind.
So Mr. and Mrs. Someone,
You better be careful who you call broken
Because you just might be one tear away
And a hurtful past does not mean
One cannot learn to love passionately today
But I'll be the first to admit,
That I do love hard
To the point where the scars may scream sometimes
But bad relationships will teach
that Loving Yourself type of love
Which you have to learn alone sometimes
So I write for those in search of it
And live to be an example for those in need of it
Because the household I grew up in taught me
What beautiful feels like.
So to those who may have had it stolen,
Especially from wolves in family's clothing,
Know your worth like the back of your hand
Know that who you love is not someone else's business
It'll come in accidents but give you tastes of perfection.
Hurt can easily make you give your trust to someone
Whose touch convinces you more than their actions
Or make you give your life over to someone
Whose words sound like they're worth dying for
But remember if a love comes with questions...
It's not the kind you deserve.
Because true love is not temporary love
So feel free to search for fairy tales and soul mates

Feel free to envision someone
who can promise you a place in history with them,
Restore a faith that not all people are meant to let you down,
Critique your dreams to have you marching on stars and,
Revise your thoughts to still believe that greatness
Can come from this Earth.
I want you to love courageously like Seventeen love
Because insecurities are repairable and yes
I do love desperately in order to minister how love
Is unconditional.

So, no, Mr. and Mrs. Someone
I didn't come from a loveless household
But I know there's no such thing as Love Professionals
So I'm willing to learn together
As we can satisfy a world hunger type of love
Because this world is starving
I see it starving
For a taste of what beautiful feels like

Thank You,
Readers, supporters, & loved ones

www.ingramcontent.com/pod-product-compliance
Lightning Source LLC
Chambersburg PA
CBHW032053040426
42449CB00007B/1090